Obedience to Sonship Call

AuthorHouse™ UK
1663 Liberty Drive
Bloomington, IN 47403 USA
www.authorhouse.co.uk
Phone: 0800.197.4150

© 2015 Ruth Rutendo Madanhi. All rights reserved.

No part of this book may be reproduced, stored in a retrieval system, or transmitted by any means without the written permission of the author.

Published by AuthorHouse 03/17/2015

ISBN: 978-1-5049-3947-8 (sc)
ISBN: 978-1-5049-3949-2 (e)

Print information available on the last page.

Any people depicted in stock imagery provided by Thinkstock are models, and such images are being used for illustrative purposes only.
Certain stock imagery © Thinkstock.

This book is printed on acid-free paper.

Because of the dynamic nature of the Internet, any web addresses or links contained in this book may have changed since publication and may no longer be valid. The views expressed in this work are solely those of the author and do not necessarily reflect the views of the publisher, and the publisher hereby disclaims any responsibility for them.

Scripture quotations marked KJV are from the Holy Bible, King James Version (Authorized Version). First published in 1611. Quoted from the KJV Classic Reference Bible, Copyright © 1983 by The Zondervan Corporation.

Contents

Acknowledgements..vii
Foreword: by Dr. Aimee Asante...ix
Introduction..xi

Chapter 1:   The Journey...1
Chapter 2:   On the Journey..7
Chapter 3:   The True Daughter..14
Chapter 4:   The Arrival..22
Chapter 5:   True Sonship call being tested........................27
Chapter 6:   True Sons & Daughters Work........................32
Chapter 7:   Finds Favour...37
Chapter 8:   Act of Obedience..41
Chapter 9:   Fruits of Obedience..46
Chapter 10: Conclusion 51

Acknowledgements

First of all I continue to thank God who gave me inspiration and revelation through His Word to write this book. Indeed our God is a good God. I also want to thank God for my loving parents and Pastors/Envoys Mr Charles and Mrs Jane Madanhi for your love and support through your prayers and teachings. May God continue to give you strength to do His will. Special thank you to my loving brothers Kudzaishe Alois Gideon and Munashe Albert Madanhi for your prayers and support. Special thank you to (mum) Netsai Dambudzo for your true love and support in my life indeed you are such a blessing to me and to the rest of the family. May the Lord Almighty continue to bless you.

My appreciation also extends to my spiritual parents in the Lord Archbishop, Apostle, Rev. Dr. Walter Masocha and Prophetess, Dr. Judith Masocha for your prayers, teachings and guidance. May the Lord continue to strengthen you as you do His will.

Team:

I would like to thank God for my lovely sister in the Lord, my mentor Dr. Aimee Asante who endured many sleepless nights editing the menuscript as well as supporting me in prayers. I continue to see the grace of God through your labour of love assisting me reach my goals in life. Thank you for being a constant pillar throughout my previous, present and I believe in future publications too. God bless you!

I extent my appreciation to my lovely sister in the Lord, Kundai Valentine Murefu who also endured sleepless nights drawing a beautiful cover illustration of this book. I continue to thank God for your support may God richly bless you. I also want to thank my dear brother in the Lord, Kudzaishe Warren Meza who also endured sleepless nights drawing a beautiful illustration also included this book. Indeed our God is faithful, God bless you! Once again, I also want to express my special thanks to my loving brother Albert Munashe Madanhi who worked tirelessly on this project particularly in photography.

Friends & Relatives around the world:

I would like to thank God for my friends and relatives around the world for your encouraging words especially in prayers. Also special thanks to Mr Vitalis & Mrs Nellie Madanhi, Agnes & Mary Madanhi, Daisy Chidamoyo, Robin Madanhi, Simbarashe & Emmanuel Chidamoyo, Kudakwashe Matapo, Netsai Murefu, Deborah Mukona, Chido Mutanikwa, Mucha Chivenga, Blessing Mashiri, Envoys/Youth Pastors Calisto & Fortunate Misi, Professor I.I & Mrs L. Dambudzo, Tsitsi, Sandra, Irean & Venanda Madanhi, Chiedza Peni, Peter Mochalski, Thelma Dewa, Gean Mukombe, Melissa Nxumalo, Patricia Musuka, (Youth Advisors) Mr Emmanuel and Mrs Patience Udogwu, Frankie Davey & Nissa Clever.

Special thank you to you the reader for taking this opportunity to read this book. God bless you!

Foreword

The first thing that strikes one about Ruth Madanhi is her quietness of spirit and the purity with which she approaches the Word of God. Her commitment to studying the Word is exemplary and a testimony to her Scripture Union background.

Ruth Madanhi is a true Ruth. She diligently pays attention to instruction, is selfless in service and always considers the impact on others, of her actions. In her book *Obedience to Sonship Call,* inspired by the book of Ruth, Ruth examines the relationship between Naomi and Ruth, extrapolating principles that could be applied by anyone under mentorship or anyone with spiritual parents, to enhance the benefits of the relationship. Ruth does not advocate blind adherence to opaque principles but systematically guides the reader through the book of Ruth, explaining the power of the principles and demonstrating a modern application. This is achieved through the exploration of themes such as submission, loyalty, humility and obedience.

The book is free from jargon, Christian-ese, and complicated theological concepts; thus, is accessible to people at all stages of their Christian walk. *Obedience to Sonship Call* is particularly relevant to those seeking to strengthen their relationship with their spiritual parents whether they are seasoned believers or new believers. It is also relevant to those seeking to understand the mechanics of such relationships and the manner in which one ought to conduct oneself. Finally, it is relevant for those whose desire is simply for a fresh look at the book of Ruth.

Dr. Aimee Asante

Image by: Kudzaishe Warren Meza

Introduction

Ruth

Ruth is the book that we find in the Bible. In this book there is an inspirational story of a lady/ woman called Ruth and her mother in law Naomi. As we read the story, we understand that she was married to one of Naomi's sons and His name was Mahlon and Orpah the other daughter in law was married to Chilion. Moreover; Naomi's husband died and she was left with her two sons and two daughters in law. They dwelt in Moab for ten years. However, time came when the two sons died and left their mother and wives.

In this book I try to highlight the importance of receiving your spiritual parent. The book captures the meaning of a *true sonship call* that we have to receive if we are to succeed in becoming who God has called us to be in the end. I believe that, it is by the grace of the Lord that He revealed this revelation to me and it has also benefited my spiritual aspect.Now time came when I started reading it again and God gave me the revelation that, the book might appear small and tiny but it carries a powerful revelation. I believe that anyone can read this same book that I'm talking about and still get a different revelation. What a Mighty God we serve. Indeed He is the God of yesterday, today and forever.

In this book *Obedience to sonship call,* I try to go through the chapters in the *book of Ruth* step by step in case someone misses the point. As I was studying the scripture I noticed that Ruth's life and Naomi had a spiritual significance or importance in the spiritual realm which is in line with what most of us are going through in our daily lives. Just to mention a few issues in relation to *spiritual sonship call: obedience, submission, loyalty, humility* and so forth have a greater impact in our lives today.

Notice that as you go through each chapter there is an important part you must grasp carefully. In other words, you shall realise that, the relationship of Naomi and Ruth was not just an ordinary relationship or connection. It was a deeper relationship that made Ruth reach her spiritual inheritance and also become part of Naomi's people. In this book *(Obedience to sonship call)*, notice that there is an important *call*; it is a call that is stirring or quickening you and me to become a true son or a true daughter of our spiritual parents. In other words, the book carries an important message for you and me, to truly yield ourselves to the vision that our spiritual parents in the Lord are carrying for our benefit. It is calling you to become part of it and stand bold as a true son or daughter who has a purpose.

Remember your life matters. It is your time, child of God, and stay under the covering of your spiritual parents. Be part of that vision that they are carrying on your behalf. To someone who wants to reconnect with your spiritual parent, it is possible. Indeed our God is the God of second chances; He is able to reconnect us. *(Luke 15:20-25)*

Begin to think deeply and be honest to yourself. For example, if God says to you, "Son or daughter, here is the direction; go that's where your blessing is." Do you think you will make it? In other words, will you be able to fulfill that call on your own? I believe that you will not make it on your own. You need your spiritual parent to be there for you. You need them to equip you so that you can start operating in a way that draws you closer to your inheritance and to the Lord. Can you imagine this; you don't need to *employ* your spiritual parent. Basically, you are not the boss or the captain. I believe any spiritual parent around the world can agree with me on this point. All spiritual parents that God blesses us with are inspired by the Holy Spirit, fully powered for excellence and Jesus Christ is their Captain. You just need to have a submissive heart to receive them in full not in part or in some measure so that, the Word which God has spoken in your life through them can be fulfilled and come to pass. You need a spiritual parent in your life. Do not be puffed up, you do need guidance.

A person can be born with a gift to become a soldier in the future, but does this mean that he or she does not need training to fulfill his or her call? I think now you are getting the idea. This person needs training so that he or she can be taught how to use the weapons, also be taught how not to run when he is needed. The person needs to learn how to receive instruction, so that he or she can defend the land. You cannot just go and join the army without being assessed and going through training. This is the reason why our spiritual parents are needed in the life of a believer. You do need to receive teachings relating to your call. You need to receive your portion.

Let me pause here by giving you a scripture in relation to the sonship call and spiritual parenting.

2 Timothy1:6, "Wherefore I put thee in remembrance that thou stir up the gift of God, which is in thee by the putting on of my hands."

As stated in the scripture I believe that for Timothy to act effectively in his call or for him to fulfill the gift which he was given by God, he still needed Apostle Paul (his spiritual father) to come and stir up that gift. Moreover, this means to quicken that gift, or Apostle Paul had to come and switch on the plug for Timothy's gift to start working effectively. On his own Timothy was not going to work in his full potential; therefore, he needed a spiritual parent to come and lay his hands on him. *Proverbs 22: 6 says, "Train up a child in the way he should go: and when he is old, he will not depart from it."*

It is a privilege for you and me at this age to get the knowledge and understanding of the importance of receiving and following teachings and instructions that we are given by our spiritual parents. It pays in the end. Let us follow them and we will be encouraged. Your children and the next generations will enjoy the benefits. So I'm saying please be blessed as you read, in fact make it a prayer in your heart to receive your spiritual parent and to be the true son or daughter.

May the Lord bless you and give you courage to fight the good fight, the fight of faith. Hallelujah. Be blessed!

Chapter 1

The Journey...

Ruth 1: 6, "Then she rose with her daughters in law, which she might return from the country of Moab: for she had heard in the country of Moab how that the Lord had visited his people giving them bread."

After the death of her two sons, Naomi decided to return to her home country (Beth-le-hem-judah).When all she had had perished she decided to return back to her own country. In other words, she knew that it was going to be her season of restoration; she knew where she was going to get her life back. Sometimes in life we get to a point when everything crumbles down as if we have come to the end of the world. But, as a child of God there is hope, there is restoration in the Lord. He is the God who revives our lives. Now, the question is how quick are you to remember? Do you remain comfortable in a terrifying situation?

In such times most of us tend to relax forgetting where we are coming from. We need someone to remind us of that which we once had from the beginning. The scripture notifies us that, Naomi knew that she was in a dead valley, a valley of death, the valley of the dry bones. I believe in her spirit she felt so weak and miserable, she was dying within. However; she kept her faith and she remembered. In other words, Naomi had a *bigger picture*. Naomi saw the *vision* and she had the vision within. Going back to her home country was the answer to her problem. I believe God spoke in her spirit and said, "Naomi you have gone through all hardship. You have been mourning for a long time, you have been living in the valley of dryness; the valley of death and now it is your season Naomi, pack your bags and go home." You might be in the same situation; the enemy might have imprisoned you, locked you from receiving your blessing in the Lord. But, the Lord is saying, "My son, my daughter go, pack your bags and leave the dry land, go to your fruitful land where you belong." Now, the question is, are you ready to take that step and move into your promised land, to the land where you belong?

Understand that the journey starts with the one who has *received* the vision. This means that the one who has received the vision knows and has got the picture of that which is ahead, Hallelujah! The one who has received the vision is fully equipped to take a step forward to receive their spiritual blessing which God has placed in their lives. No matter what the visionary might be faced with, come thunder and come rain; he or she is ready to move into his or her rightful place. He or she has seen the *bigger picture* ahead of them, and I believe that any true woman or man of God understands that they cannot miss out or cannot *afford* to miss out that which is ahead of them. They can't sit down comfortably when they know that there is something great waiting for them, Hallelujah! In other words, it is actually unwise for them to remain in that position, because they have already seen that which is ahead. They have seen the fat land; they have seen the green land filled with milk and honey. Only prosperity is ahead and is waiting for them.

I believe no one wants to remain on the same level, especially when the Lord has shown a bigger picture. You have to see, open your eyes to see that which is bigger than your natural senses can imagine. If you can see it, then you can be it. You cannot move from one point to another if you haven't seen the picture. The way you perceive things has a greater effect in your life. It is not just about seeing the picture, but what you *remember* as well. This means that what you recall impacts your life decisions. Understand that as human beings we also remember some events, and this helps us to familiarise ourselves with situations attached to our environment.

So, as we read the story we find out that Naomi remembered. If you can at this time, just say it loud that, "Naomi *remembered*." She remembered her country. According to some studies, her country Bethlehem was and is an agricultural land. This means that she belonged to a fruitful land. Naomi remembered her land. When you know who you are and who you represent, then nothing should attack you spiritually, physically, emotionally, socially and intellectually. The reason is that you are not ignorant; you know where to go when you are surrounded with deep misery of life. When you know how big your problem is, then you know the bigger solution to it. This is amazing indeed. Our God is the Problem Solver, therefore; there is nothing too hard for God to solve. He is the Mighty Warrior, the King of kings; He is the King of Glory. *(Psalm24)*. If you are a child of God, it is very important for you to know where to go and whom to turn to in times of difficulty. Know who your God is and know whom you should cry.

Naomi lost her husband but, not just her husband, also her two married sons. In the natural we say Naomi lost her *all*. Naomi lost all that she treasured most but, I want you to believe with me that Naomi *had it all*. Let me repeat it here again that, "Naomi had it all." In the spiritual realm she had all that she required. I think after all the adversaries that she encountered in her life she might have said, "Ah, this God has turned His face away from me so why can't I worship other *gods* who can understand my circumstance." I want you to begin to understand how faithful she was to stick to the same God who was with her when she moved to the land of Moab and was still with her when she was returning back to her home country. His grace, your faithfulness to the Lord keeps you closer to Him. She might have stayed and endured the hardship, but she decided to *reposition* herself. She might have become more proud and decided to stay and mourn all her life.

Times like these, we prefer to suffer and endure the pain thinking that's life and that is the way it should be. Let me remind you of this: mourning may endure for a night, but joy comes in the morning, *Psalm 30: 5*. There is joy waiting for you. Rise up, pack your bags and go to your fruitful land. The enemy rejoices when you are in pain, in bondage and stressed all your life. Listen, he attacks you more when he knows that you are in a hectic situation. In other words, he comes to steal your fruitful and powerful thoughts of increase and prosperity in your life, by attacking your mind. Just think of it, Naomi was surrounded with all these stressful situations in her life. I believe her mind was dying as well, simply because of the events she had gone through.

According *to 2 Corinthians 10:4-5,*

"For the weapons of our warfare are not carnal, but mighty through God to the pulling down of strongholds; (5) Casting down imaginations, and everything that exalted itself against the knowledge of God, and bringing in to captivity every thought to the obedience of Christ."

Our weapons are not carnal; our weapons are not fleshly made, but mighty through God to the pulling down of strongholds. These *strongholds* are satanic attacks or forces that the enemy brings to hold the children of God from moving in God's purpose. The aim of the wicked one is to remove you from your goals so that you cannot achieve your spiritual inheritance in the Lord. Praise be to the Most High that our weapons are not carnal, but are mighty through God, not through idols, or any other god you can think of, but mighty through God, The Almighty God, The King of Glory, Hallelujah!

Through Christ, The Way, The Truth and The Life, we can cast those strongholds down to the obedience of God. Listen obedience to God, Obedience to God not to man, not to idols, but to God. I believe you might be wondering what exactly I want to put forward to you. Let us consider this part very carefully.

When Naomi, decided to go to her home land, her decision was the *root or an act of obedience* to the Lord. Her first step was to *obey*; I believe every true man or woman of God around the world can confirm this. A true visionary is obedient. Why am I saying this?

Psalm 37: 23-24, "The steps of a good man are ordered by the Lord: and he delighteth in his way. (24) Though he fall, he shall not be utterly cast down: for the Lord upholdeth him with his hand."

The decision to go back to her country was not just an ordinary step she took, it was by divine order or assignment, I can say. It was not just a natural move for her to decide; I'm now packing my bags and going back to my country." I believe that Naomi felt the *call* deep within and it caused her not to remain in the same position. She must have heard the voice of the Lord speaking within her spirit calling her to her spiritual destiny. According to Dr. Walter Masocha, *Threshing Floor D.I.Y Style: A New Approach for a New Generation; From Harvest to Seed, 2013,* "Whatever obtains in the physical is only a mirror or reflection of what happens in the spiritual." In other words, Naomi's decision wasn't just operating in the physical, but it was based in the spiritual.

Why her decision?...

Proverbs 4: 8, "But the path of the just is as the shining light, that shinneth more and more unto the perfect day."

Her decision to be obedient to the call, made it possible for her to walk in her spiritual plan which God had prepared already for her (*in due season*). Moreover, she remembered the land, (she saw the greenness, the fruitful picture). Naomi saw revival deep within. She saw that which was ahead of her. Naomi received the call and made a step of obedience in her life, not just her only, but for the *generations* to come. *The foundation of progress.* One step of obedience changed her life and the generations to come. Only one step of acceptance turned her sorrows to joy.

Chapter 2

On the Journey...

I understand that most people are so familiar with this beautiful story. Some prefer it as a love *(romance)* story because of the end results of obedience to the call. Well! Allow me to go through the story step by step, I believe that our God, we serve, is also the God of revelations, moreover, God reveals His messages to us in various ways. So, child of God fasten your seat belt, we are on a journey. Let us delve deeper into the story.

Ruth 1:7, "Wherefore she went forth out of the place where she was, and her two daughters in law with her; and they went on the way to return unto the land of Judah.

Naomi decided to return to the land of Judah, her home country and her two daughters in law also followed her. They were together on the journey. Let me remind you again, it was a journey.

Finding out who is the true *son* or true daughter?

Again, allow me to remind you that we are on a journey.

Ruth 1: 8, "And Naomi said unto her two daughters in law, Go, return each to her mother's house: the Lord deal kindly with you, as ye have dealt with the dead, and with me. (9) The Lord grant you that ye may find rest, each of you in the house of husband. Then she kissed them; and they lifted up their voice and wept. (10) And they said unto her, Surely we will return with thee unto thy people. (11) And Naomi said, Turn again, my daughters: why will ye go with me? Are there yet any more sons in my womb, that ye may be your husbands? (12) Turn again my daughters, go your way; for I am too old to have an husband. If I should say, I have hope, if I should have an husband also to night, and should also bear sons; (13) Would ye tarry for them till they were grown? Would ye say for them from having husbands? Nay, my daughters; for it grieveth me much for your sakes that the hand of the Lord is gone out against me.

The one who has the vision; he or she is the one who has received the bigger picture. As we said earlier, the vision is not ordinary. It is a unique vision for the *true*; let me say this again, the TRUE sons and daughters. Hallelujah! According to the scripture, Naomi with her two daughters in law, Ruth and Orpah were now on a journey to the land of Judah. Let me take you back, Ruth and Orpah were Moabites and Naomi their mother in law was an Israelite, in other words she belonged to the land of Judah.

Let us take it this way, Naomi was in the position of a *spiritual parent* of the *real or true daughter.* You will find out why, I mentioned daughter instead of daughters in the next segment of the chapter. I believe something stirred Naomi's heart and said, "Naomi, you need to be in agreement with the ones you are travelling with on this journey." Something touched her heart; maybe she felt so heavy deep within. She might have felt as if she was holding someone's freedom. *The heart of a true spiritual parent,* Naomi had to stop and obey that still voice that was crying deep within.

Remember on a journey, you have to stop and check your vehicle to determine that everything is still functioning well. As you are reading, just take few minutes or seconds and have a glass of water, refresh your mind.

Back on the move.

Ruth 1: 8, "And Naomi said unto her two daughters in law, Go, return each to her mother's house: the Lord deal kindly with you, as ye have dealt with the dead, and with me. (9) The Lord grant you that ye may find rest, each of you in the house of husband. Then she kissed them; and they lifted up their voice and wept. (10) And they said unto her, Surely we will return with thee unto thy people. (11) And Naomi said, Turn again, my daughters: why will ye go with me? Are there yet any more sons in my womb, that ye may be your husbands? (12) Turn again my daughters, go your way; for I am too old to have an husband. If I should say, I have hope, if I should have an husband also to night, and should also bear sons; (13) Would ye tarry for them till they were grown? Would ye say for them from having husbands? Nay, my daughters; for it grieveth me much for your sakes that the hand of the Lord is gone out against me.

Naomi stopped; Naomi obeyed. Read carefully the scripture above. Begin to understand her warm and loving words to her daughters in law. Remember, Naomi is representing a spiritual parent. A *spiritual parent*, is there to give you counsel (instruction, correction). They are there to edify your spiritual being in reaching your call to become who God has called you to be. Moreover, they carry bountiful blessings for your benefit, through offering spiritual mentorship, helping you to receive that which God has planned and prepared for you. They are there to carry you on their wings so that you can fly on high levels. They are there to teach you to become the real person you are supposed to be. Furthermore, their wisdom concerning your life are not naturally or fleshly based but spiritually based.

You are spiritually birthed by your spiritual parents in the spiritual realm. Your actions towards situations and so forth can tell whose child are you. The seed of obedience produces its fruit, and the seed of disobedience produces its own. It is just a gentle reminder that you understand that you are a reflection of your spiritual parent through your actions and so forth. This doesn't necessarily mean that you are in the position of your spiritual parent. Understand me on this one, because many confuse this part and the end result is that they may think highly forgetting where they have received the anointing from. If you are a true daughter or a true son, then this means that you have received an *impartation* from your spiritual mother or father in the Lord. Moreover, you have taken or received a part of not the whole of it. Remember it's called im*part* so it is the *part of* the anointing not the *whole of it*, Hallelujah! Glory to God!

For example, in the book of 1Kings 19:19-21 and 2 Kings 2:9 we hear the story of Elijah and Elisha. God revealed to Elijah that he was going to anoint Elisha to become a prophet.

1Kings 19: 19-21

"So he departed thence, and found Elisha the son of Shaphat, who was plowing with twelve yoke of oxen before him, and he with the twelfth: and <u>Elijah passed by him, and cast his mantle upon him.</u> (20) And he left the oxen, and ran after Elijah, and said, Let me, I pray thee, kiss my father and my mother, and then I will follow thee. And he said unto him, Go back again: for what have I done to thee? (21) And he returned back from him, and took a yoke of oxen, and slew them, and boiled their flesh with the instruments of the oxen, and gave unto the people, and they did eat. Then he arose, and went after Elijah, and ministered to him."

Elijah anointed Elisha as he was instructed by God. Moreover, when Elijah passed the mantle to Elijah, I believe at that time he still needed to be prepared for the greater task ahead. However, Elisha needed to grow under the spiritual mentorship of Elijah and receive teachings concerning his call. According to the scripture we realise that Elisha had to follow Elijah so that he could receive more counsel. Since Elisha had already received his portion of the anointing (passing of the mantle), I believe at that time he had only received the *part of* the impartation not the *whole of it*. The next scripture explains why.

2 Kings 2:8-14

"And Elijah took his mantle, and wrapped it together, and smote the waters, and they were divided hither and thither, so that they two went over on dry ground. (9) <u>And it came to pass, when they were gone over, that Elijah said unto Elisha, Ask what I shall do for thee before I be taken away from thee. And Elisha said, I pray thee, let a double portion of thy spirit be upon me.</u> (10) And he said, Thou hast asked a hard thing: nevertheless, if thou see me when I am taken from thee, it shall be so unto thee; but if not, it shall not be so. (11) And it came to pass, as they still went on, and talked, that, behold, there appeared a chariot of fire, and horses of fire, and parted them both asunder; and Elijah went up by a whirlwind into heaven. (12)

And Elisha saw it, and he cried, My father, my father, the chariot of Isreal, and the horsemen thereof. And he saw him no more: and he took hold of his own clothes, and rent them in two pieces. (13) <u>He took up also the mantle of Elisha that fell on him,</u> and went back, and stood by the bank of Jordan;"

The scripture above suggest that it was time for Elijah to go and he asked Elisha what he wanted him to do for him. Elisha asked for a double portion of the spirit that was upon Elijah. I believe that Elisha was now prepared for the great task ahead of him and it was now time for him request for the full impartation that was upon Elijah since he was not going to be with him during ministry.

Morover, this suggest that Elisha was now ready to receive the whole impartation since he was now Elijah's *successor*. In addition, Elisha received his double portion under the leadership of his spiritual father Elijah as he was going to continue the ministry as the Lord had ordained.

Now we have discussed about a *spiritual parent*. Let us move on now, I believe that Naomi knew who her true daughter was already, she just wanted to make sure she set the other free who was not connected or attached to the vision. She had to make sure that she had taken the right seed, Hallelujah! It was the seed that was going to produce greater things. She had to take the best. Now the question is, how was she going to take the best and how was she going to know that this is the best seed that is going to produce greater things to come?

Naomi stopped, and she said to her daughters go your ways, and she also gave them some reasons why it was good for them to go their desired ways. I believe at this point Naomi was crying within, saying, "Oh my, my, how am I going to travel on my own if both decide to go their ways. I shall be on my own. Oh! I have no one to hold on to. My children just died and my husband too, oh! God why me?" Just think of it, nowadays, we have buses, trains and cars for travelling purposes. Back in those days there was nothing like that only horses and you were even blessed to have one. I understand that Naomi and the two daughters in law had to travel on foot. Can you imagine, Oh! How blessed are we this generation.

Naomi gave the ladies the chance to do what they desired. Though she had a bigger picture, she knew the land very well. She was the visionary of that vision. But the question still stands, who was the *true daughter* of that *vision*? Is it Ruth or Orpah? Let us find out in the next chapter, it's a journey!

Chapter 3

The True Daughter...

Ruth 1: 14, "And they lifted up their voice, and wept again: and Orpah kissed her mother in law; but Ruth clave unto her. (15) And she said, Behold, thy sister in law is gone back unto her people, and unto her gods: return thou after thy sister in law. (16) And Ruth said, Intreat me not to leave thee, or to return from following after thee: for thou longest, I will lodge: they people shall be my people, and thy God my God: (17) Where thou diest, I will die, and there will I be buried: the Lord do so to me, and more also, if ought but death part thee and me.

The scripture clearly states Orpah and Ruth's responses after their mother in law had kindly asked them to return to their mother's house and start a new life.

Orpah...

After she had heard and received her mother in law's kind words she turned back, and went away fulfilling her desired purpose that she had purposed already. Notice that, when someone is not a true son or daughter, they simply hear the words and quickly turn back without any delay, because within they no longer feel comfortable to be part of the journey. In other words, they have reached their destination. Let us take it this way, as you know, we all travel different places around the world. Sometimes we can be on a journey that is not destined for us, so to make it easier, we find out that we simply change the route and go back to where we had purposed to go before.

In this story, you find that Orpah, who was not attached to the vision, simply turned back and went away. She didn't need anyone to tell her to stop and cleave to Naomi since she was her mother in law. Orpah knew what she wanted; therefore her decision led her the way to her original home she belonged to.

Indeed Naomi proved to be a wise woman; she knew it was a good thing to give her daughters a sense of freedom. She allowed them to make their choices. However, this then brings us to the subject or teaching that I have learned from the man of God Dr, Walter Masocha, *"Salvation is personal, or Salvation as a life time decision."* Naomi had to make sure that the ladies have chosen their paths freely, so that they will not blame her from following her original plan or her vision she had. Your decision matters, ask yourself if your decisions do uplift, motivate or bring positive results in your life.

Your decision has an impact on your being. It either destroys you or produces greater things. So you have got to be very careful with the decisions you make in life. Remember one decision can change your life for better or for worse. Orpah decided to worship her *gods* as stated in the scripture; those gods are associated with *idol worship*. Ruth 1:15, *"And she said, Behold, thy sister in law is gone back unto her people, and unto her gods: return thou after thy sister in law."* As a child of God I believe you now understand what it means. Orpah returned to her old ways, old life style, character, her old ways of thinking, old ways of associations, and also relationships she had.

I'm just wondering what kind of a relationship she had with Naomi before she returned back to her home village. What was her relationship with Naomi? In addition, was it a *relationship* or an *association* kind of connection?

I believe if she had a true relationship with her mother in law she would have stayed and been willing enough to receive major blessings through her. Well! Who am I to judge the decision she made? It was her path, and she fulfilled her part.

Ruth...

Proverbs 16: 24, "Pleasant words are as an honeycomb, sweet to the soul, and health to the bones."

The response of a true daughter speaks of revival, restoration, the renewal of mind and soul. Ruth's response calmed her mother in law. I believe spiritual fathers and mothers around the world can agree with me. When a true daughter or son is willing to drop all their treasures in life or humble themselves into following the plan or the vision which their spiritual parents have received from the Lord, you can just tell. Their actions and words can prove if they are part of and also agreeing with the call upon their spiritual parents. Since a spiritual son or daughter received an impartation or part of the portion of the anointing from their spiritual parents, they automatically see the picture ahead. They might not see the bigger picture naturally or physically with their naked eyes but, something has been deposited into their spirit (the inner man). And it is attached to them in the spiritual realm. So, they can receive the word and have the courage to stay in line with the vision or that which God has for them through their spiritual parents. Understand that the power of God works, whether big or small, it works.

True sons or daughters are spiritually and physically *rooted* in the vision. Come thunder and come rain, they will stand by their spiritual parents and strengthen them in difficulty. *Humility, obedience, ownership* of the vision and the visionary is their portion.

Ruth chose to follow the God of Naomi, who is the King of kings, Hallelujah! It is amazing indeed. Ruth could have followed Orpah's path, but she made her decision, she purposed a purpose that she would follow the God of her mother in law. She knew where her blessing was. She had a relationship with her mother in law, not just as a mother in law but as her spiritual mother. I believe that, before her husband Mahlon died, Ruth used to go and visit her mother in law more often and even more when her husband passed away. Ruth could spend more time fellowshipping with her mother in law, as well as hearing stories of her home country and other testimonies. Ruth knew her mother and the mother knew her.

Ruth had a relationship with her mother to the extent that she didn't want to remain in her *old ways*; she wanted to abide with her. Naomi was her family and she was her *all*. This means that Ruth knew from her spirit that for her to excel to another level, for her to mount up with wings as the eagles she needed her spiritual mother (Naomi). Already Ruth was blessed, all she required was within her, but she needed a spiritual mother to open that door of progress and usher her into a new phase of life. Life without limits.

True sons and daughters love guidance and embrace instructions from their spiritual parents. They pay attention to their voice and listen.

As we read the scripture carefully, Ruth was actually signing a contract with her mother in law that she was going to follow her wherever she goes. You might be wondering, why I said she was signing a *contract*. Ruth was committed to following her mother in law wherever she goes, simply by pouring her heart or saying that which was in her inner-most part of her heart. Futhermore, Ruth made a *vow*. What an act of true love and compassion Ruth proved to her mother in law.

By expressing such words it lightened her mother in law's heart. Let us find out her mother in law's response to such powerful and moving words of love. Let me remind you that, Ruth wasn't just saying these words to prove her holiness or to show off, that she was more perfect than Orpah. As we said earlier Ruth had a *relationship* with her mother; therefore, expressing such words wasn't a problem at all because it was her *language* already, it was in her already. Moreover, this was her natural way of communicating with her mother, which basically tells us that it wasn't something new. It was her life, it was her life style; therefore, she didn't require any lesson or further instruction on how she was going to respond to such a situation. *Sonship call rooted and grounded in her.*

Ruth knew the importance of staying under the *covering*. Psalm 84: 11, "<u>For the Lord God is a sun and shield</u>: the Lord will give grace and glory: <u>no good thing will he withhold from them that walk uprightly</u>." The *covering*, here represent the shelter, shield, anointing of God placed upon her mother in law (her spiritual mother Naomi), that she had to benefit or partake from. This coverage or covering was only available for her as long as she remained under her spiritual mother. This means that if Ruth decided to follow Orpah, she was going to depart from the anointing. As long as she stayed under her mother in law, Ruth was ready to receive that which belonged to her physically and spiritually.

At this time you might be saying, "There is nothing bad that Orpah did, in leaving her mother in law." Well! I can agree with you, but just listen carefully. The scripture doesn't tell us anything what happened to Orpah when she left her mother in law. We don't even know whether she reached where she was going safely. I believe you can agree with me on this one. When Orpah was with her mother in law Naomi, she was mentioned. Only the time she *turned back* we never heard anything about her life and any progress that came after her decision she made.

Ruth 1: 15, "And she said Behold, thy sister in law is gone back unto her people, and unto her gods: return thou after thy sister in law."

Moreover, the scripture notifies us that Orpah returned back to her gods and this indicate that she chose failure instead of receiving the Almighty God in her life. However, she did not avail herself to be used for God's purpose at that particular time. Orpah wasn't ready to follow her mother in law, additionally she chose her natural desires. Her desire led her to her destiny. She only desired what she thought was best for her, she considered herself more highly. The importance of *loyalty*. Orpah was not loyal enough to consider her mother in law. This means that she only thought the best for herself and forgetting others who were with her from the beginning. She decided to do her own thing she thought was good. Just think of her desire.... She desired the god (idol worship) However, there is no indication that she was led by God. *Ruth 1: 15, "And she said Behold, thy sister in law is gone back unto her people, and unto her gods: return thou after thy sister in law."* She didn't have a bigger vision of what she was supposed to receive through her mother in law Naomi. She chose death, whereas Ruth desired life.

The decision she made took her to her destiny. Orpah refused to follow the true God of all the earth. She decided to worship her gods; she decided to go back to her old life. Just think of it, a person running

Obedience to Sonship Call

away from life by choosing death. Idol worship (gods), are associated with death, simply because those who worship such have a relationship with a dead or a non-living thing. Let us get this right; what do you get from worshiping a non-living thing that doesn't create any living thing. You are a living creature; therefore you are even more powerful. Why reduce yourself by bowing and raising your hands to a non-living thing? You have the real God, the Creator of the heavens and earth. Do not be blinded. Follow the Living God. He is the one who answers by fire. He is the God of Miracles, the God of Signs and Wonders.

Ruth 1:18, "When she saw that she was steadfastly minded to go with her, then she left speaking unto her."

As we said earlier on, that you can just tell if a person is your spiritual daughter or son, by the way they respond to situations. True sons and daughters stick to their spiritual parents, they follow their instruction. After all that was said, Naomi couldn't stop Ruth from following her, because Ruth had purposed in her heart that she would remain rooted to her mother in law. She was well dedicated or obedient to the *sonship call* she had received within. I would like to believe that Ruth followed her mother in law instructions, may be her mother in law would send her to buy some vegetables at a supermarket and she would return with the change and give it back to her. Ruth's response, was fully packed with maturity, in other words she carried herself as a woman of wisdom. She was wise to make a decision that connected her even more to her mother in law (spiritual mother Naomi).

In the book of Ruth chapter one, the scripture informs us that Naomi came from the land of Judah. However, Ruth transformed from a Moabite in the spiritual and become part of Judah. I hope you are getting the meaning. By committing herself to following her mother in law, Ruth received a portion of Judah. In addition, you cannot partake of the portion without the willingness of heart of *commitment*. A *submissive* heart prepares you to receive your blessing. To receive the portion you must yield yourself to the vision through your spiritual parent (the one who has received the vision, the visionary). Ruth had to be submissive to her spiritual mother Naomi. Let us focus now on her words she expressed to her mother.

Ruth 1: (16) And Ruth said, Intreat me not to leave thee, or to return from following after thee: for thou lodgest, I will lodge: they people shall be my people, and thy God my God: (17) Where thou diest, I will die, and there will I be buried: the Lord do so to me, and more also, if ought but death part thee and me.

The scripture goes on to say that, *she was steadfastly.* This means that Ruth was strong enough, courageous, and unmovable, simply rooted and grounded to that which she had purposed in her heart. She refused to turn back to idol worship. I believe even in her heart she was saying, "Ah! I also want to experience; I also want to walk with this God whom my mother in law worships. I also want to partake of the blessing, I want to be part of the tribe of Judah, I have heard great testimonies, and I want to have a relationship with this God she serves. I have heard that He is the Living God the Creator of the universe, so I have made up my mind to follow this God."

You cannot follow something without the hunger to receive more of it. Remember what happened at that well in Samaria. *(John 4:11-15)* After having an encounter with Jesus Christ, the woman of Samaria was now thirsty for the *Living Waters* she had heard about, and she wanted to receive the *Living Waters* (Jesus Christ in her spirit). When you have heard of the Good News, you cannot afford to stay on the same level; you want to experience that which is ahead of you. You begin to desire a relationship with the Great I am. Maybe you have heard someone testify of what the Lord has done in his or her life, maybe they should have died before in an accident, but something, somehow happened. Someone saved their lives, Jesus Christ saved their lives, and you now desire the same Jesus Christ who saved their lives too. You want that connection in your life. So the question is; what do you desire?

John 14:6, "Jesus saith unto him, I am the way, the truth, and the life: no man cometh unto the Father, but by me."

You better be part of the Kingdom, that's where you can get all that you require. Refuse to be in darkness; don't run away from the light.

Chapter 4
The Arrival...

Ruth 1:19, "So they two went until they came to Beth-ele-hem. And it came to pass, when they were come to Beth-le-hem, that all the city was moved about them, and they said, Is this Naomi? (20) And she said unto them, Call me not Naomi, call me Mara: for the Almighty hath dealt very bitterly with me. (21) I went out full, and the Lord hath brought me home again empty: why then call ye Naomi, seeing the Lord hath testified against me, and the Almighty hath afflicted me?

The above scripture states that Naomi and Ruth arrived in the land of Bethlehem and people were greatly moved or excited about their arrival. Remember as we read the story in the beginning we hear that Naomi sojourned in the country of Moab with her husband and her two sons, though they later on passed away. The scripture also goes on to say, Naomi said, "I went out full, and the Lord hath brought me home again empty, why then call ye Naomi, seeing the Lord hath testified against me, and the Almighty hath afflicted me?" I wonder why Naomi was saying such words, in return to their excitement. I believe Naomi was just touched by the way she lost her husband and the two children in the foreign land (Moab). Maybe before she thought she would return home with her family and rejoice greatly with her people in Bethlehem, but it didn't happen that way.

Well! I assume that Ruth was just standing beside her mother in law, just wondering if she meant what she was saying. Seeing that everyone in the city was in great joy celebrating the arrival of Naomi, I believe something quickened the people in the city. It was a time of celebration. Naomi has arrived home.

There are times in life when you would have arrived at a place of revival, but deep within you are not sure if you do deserve the joy that is welcoming you. You arrive at a certain place, and you are not sure whether to rejoice with them that are celebrating your arrival. Oh! I can hear everyone in the city singing welcoming songs, songs of joy and restoration, saying, "Naomi you have made it, Naomi rejoice, it is your new season of major breakthroughs, rejoice Naomi rejoice." But all this wasn't making any sense to Naomi, because she had the *old picture* of what happened before. She was hurt deep within that she couldn't dance to the songs of joy that her people were singing in celebration of her coming.

I believe at this time, each time Naomi wanted to smile, the old event would come on her mind and say, "Ah! Naomi remember where you are coming from. Your husband died, your two sons also and Orpah returned to her people." I understand that there are times in life when God blesses you with a new life and a new beginning but the old or past experience will try obscuring your vision. However; these are the strongholds that attack your purpose in reaching your destiny. Instead of rejoicing and forgetting all the sorrows you have gone through, the enemy still expects you to be destroyed and truly crushed so that you won't get up and walk in God's destiny for your life. You can hear the sound of joy, many people cheering you up for victory saying, "You have made it! Yes! You have made it!" But still an obstacle will appear on your pathway so that you remain in bondage. The enemy wants you dead, so that you won't get to where God expects you to be.

The weapons of our warfare are not carnal, but mighty through God, Hallelujah! Celebrate when your life is being lifted up from the dunghill. Remember what happened to Joseph, He was thrown in the pit. He was expected to die in there so that he could not reach his destiny, which God had ordained for His life. If God has opened the door of success in your life, don't sit down, and worry again, begin to celebrate God's grace upon your life. When He opens that gate of progress, rejoice because it is your new season. Behold, all things have become new, the old has passed away. (2 Corinthians 5:17)

Isaiah 43:18-19, "Remember ye not the former things, neither consider the things of old. Behold, I will do a new thing; now it shall spring forth; shall ye not know it? I will even make a way in the wilderness, and rivers in the desert."

You are starting a new chapter in your life. Oh! Hallelujah! What a Mighty God we serve.

Do not look back. Remember Naomi and Ruth had to travel a long way, I don't know how many days they took, but they had to go on a journey. A journey is a process of revival. Why revival? You are meant to forget all your sorrows and simply move forward with a rejoicing heart. This may not apply to all journeys in life. However, in this context a journey keeps you in line with what God has in stored for you. It might also mean that, Naomi decided to leave the old life, a life full of hardship; therefore, shifting position is another means of showing progress in life. When you are tired of remaining on the same level you pack your bags and go. You *reposition* as a way of telling yourself that there are greater things ahead of me; there is something waiting for me. So, celebrate when God brings you to a new land, Hallelujah!

When I was reading this scripture something just touched my heart. Bear in mind that Ruth made a vow that she was not going to leave her mother in law. However; this basically means that Ruth was now part of Naomi; she was her relative, her own (people). Ruth is now Naomi's daughter not just daughter in law. Understand that from the previous chapter we discussed that Ruth signed a contract, meaning that she is now part of Naomi, she belongs to Naomi.

Well! The scripture states that Naomi said, "I went out full, and the Lord hath brought me home again *empty.*" Let us get this right. How come Naomi is saying to her own people she came back home *empty*? I can assume that she might have been referring to a parcel of thanksgiving to offer her people... never know, obviously we understand that she lost her husband and two sons. Naomi arrived in the land with her daughter in law, not just that but her spiritual daughter Ruth. Remember that Ruth was there when Naomi was saying such words to her people, can you imagine. Listen to this, Ruth didn't say to her mother in law in front of the people, "Ah! Mum how come you are saying such words, can't you see I am here with you and we have travelled together throughout the journey, and this is what you are now saying to your people. Why are you rude like this? You can't even see that I walked with you I should have gone with Orpah who returned to her people, but I sacrificed to stay with you." Oh! My, my Ruth could have just said such words, but she kept her dignity and loyalty. She did not question her spiritual mother. She *maintained* her *sonship call.* If Ruth questioned her spiritual mother she might have misbehaved or acted rebelliously towards her mother. However, she had to remain silent at that time as a manner of showing respect. In addition, her silence created a peaceful environment rather than creating a conflict.

Proverbs 16: 23, "The heart of the wise teacheth his mouth, and addeth learning to his lips."

Let us find out why in the next chapter.

Chapter 5

True Sonship call being tested...

Ruth 2: 1, "And Naomi had a kinsman of her husband's a mighty man of wealth, of the family of Elimelech; and his name was Boaz. (2) And Ruth the Moabitess said unto Naomi, Let me now go to the field, and glean ears of corn after him in whose sight I shall find grace. And she said unto her, Go, my daughter.

When both Naomi and Ruth had arrived in the land Bethlehem, the scripture states that they came in the land in the beginning of barley harvest. It was a rich country indeed. Remember Ruth and her spiritual mother was coming from Moab where they lost all that they treasured in their lives. But they decided to go back to the country of restoration.

As we said earlier on in the previous chapter that Ruth didn't question her spiritual mother when she said that she came back empty. Allow me to explain this to you. Naomi could have told her people that, "I now have a daughter. See everyone! This is what the Lord has blessed me with during my struggle and the loss that I experienced."

True daughters and true sons look for opportunity.

Ruth 2:3, "And she went, and came, and gleaned in the field after the reapers: and her harp was to light on part of the field belonging unto Boaz, who was of the kindred of Elimelech."

Ruth saw the need. She noticed that there was a task that was supposed to be accomplished. Though she knew that she was Naomi's spiritual daughter, she knew that she was supposed to look for something to do. Understand that for Ruth to come out of Moab, it was through her spiritual mother. She is the one who made it possible for her to come to Bethlehem the land of Judah. Bear in mind that Ruth didn't just wake up and say, "Mother let us go to Bethlehem that is where my blessing is." Ruth knew nothing on her own, but through Naomi she managed to go to the land of Judah. Remember that Ruth was originally a Moabite and Naomi was an Israelite she belonged to Judah.

The scripture notifies us that Naomi was related to Boaz simply because he was a kinsman of her husband of the family of Elimelech. Ruth couldn't prosper on her own without her spiritual mother. In other words, though she was not originally a citizen of that land where there was a great harvest this didn't mean that Ruth had to cut her relationship with her spiritual mother Naomi. Their relationship had to be firm. Without Naomi there was no opportunity for Ruth.

Ruth might have arrived in that great country and told her spiritual mother that she was no longer continuing with her anymore. She could have departed from her and done something else to free herself from Naomi's leadership. But, Ruth continued with her spiritual mother, she stayed under her covering.

Notice that Ruth didn't just go to work in the fields without consulting her spiritual mother. Immediately after she had seen the need for workers in the field, Ruth could not wait; she informed her spiritual mother that she wanted to work in the field. Maybe you have arrived in that land where there is a great harvest, but are you willing to work and support the vision? The vision to build a new generation that is zealous for the things of God. Ruth maintained her loyalty; she was humble enough to work in the fields.

I believe that most of you can agree on this one. Many a times we get blessed but we forget our loyalty to God, and start serving our own personal desires. These are the things that only satisfy our hearts and minds only. We start caring more about ourselves than doing what

God expects us to do. We sit back and relax when we get blessed. All that we want is the praise of being called daughters and sons but not willing to step up and work even harder to fulfill what we are supposed to. We want to enjoy the benefits, but not willing to yield ourselves to the task ahead of us. Indeed the harvest is plenty but the labourers are few, *Matthew 9: 37-38.*

Being called a son or a daughter means that you are a *worker*. Hard work is in your bones; therefore, it is not new in your system. It has been planted within. All you need to have is the heart to work. It is your duty to do the task before it expires.

Begin to see God's true sons and true daughters looking for opportunity; they don't wait for someone to give them something to do. Instead of enjoying the benefits of the sonship titles they take advantage of the opportunity available for them. They are not lazy, but they grab the chance they have and do something.

True daughters and sons are known by their *ability to serve*. They don't enjoy the titles and enjoy the benefits of the palace when they are seated doing nothing at all, but they embrace opportunities and do the work.

Remember that the field belonged to Boaz who was also related to Naomi. Ruth held on to her vow she made to her spiritual mother. She got the picture that Boaz was related to Naomi; therefore Boaz is automatically counted to be Ruth's people too. After she was told, I believe that Ruth was now telling herself that, "I am now here in this land and it will be an honour to work in the fields in appreciation of what my spiritual mother has done in my life. She brought me into this country, and I am now in the land of Judah and I can now *connect* myself to this Living God."

Ruth took a step of sonship, she was willing to work. Moreover, she humbled herself to the extent of becoming a servant. Becoming a servant requires your submission to the authority or those above you. You simply break your fleshly desires, by paying attention to that which is surrounding you and you are willing to contribute something. Ruth was willing to sweat. Maybe she could have said, "But other young women out there are going out with their friends busy shopping and having KFC or Nandos, but I'm stuck in the fields busy working and sweating here."

Bear in mind that it was also sunny, I believe that it wasn't that easy. Ruth endured, she was a hard worker. Maybe she could have stayed with her spiritual mother all day discussing why she told her people that she wanted to be called Mara at that time. Ruth could have sat at home busy painting her nails trying to impress the men in that land of Bethlehem. She could have said, "Ah! I need a new hair style, I need to change my identity so that I can be recognised or someone can approach me.

Ruth was a *wise* woman, she was a *virtuous* woman. She was a woman of dignity and of a noble character. Wisdom was her clothing. She was a worker. *Proverbs 31*

Chapter 6

True Sons & Daughters Work...

Ruth 2: 4, "And, behold, Boaz came from Beth-le-hem, and said unto the reapers, The Lord be with you. And they answered him, The Lord bless thee. (5) Then said Boaz unto his servant that was set over the reapers, Whose damsel is this? (6) And the servant that was set over the reapers answered and said, It is the Moabitish damsel that came back with Naomi out of the country of Moab: (7) And she said, I pray you, let me glean and gather after the reapers among the sheaves: so she came, and hath continued even from the mourning until now, that she tarried a little in the house

The moment Ruth decided to go and work in the fields forgetting that she was just coming from Moab her home country, she did not treat herself as a visitor or a guest simply because she was a Moabite. She was quick to join others who were working in the fields. If you are a worker you don't need someone to remind you that there is so much work that needs to be done. You make sure that you are available in case you miss out on your blessing when others receive their portion.

As we have discussed in the previous chapter that Ruth was a worker, she was not lazy. Bear in mind Ruth wasn't familiar with the environment, in other words she knew no one in that city. You can imagine, you have been employed at a work place and you notice that you don't even know anyone in that company. What do you do in this situation? You see everyone laughing and chatting whilst working and you are on your own. I can assume that you begin to feel isolated. All you want to do is to finish your shift and go back home and have a rest. Oh! What a strong woman she was. As stated in the scripture above, Boaz saw Ruth working in his field and went on to ask his servant who she was and the reason why she joined everyone else. So, his servant informed him about the *damsel* (Ruth) how she came and kindly asked to work saying, *"I pray you, let me glean and gather after the reapers among the sheaves, continued even from the morning until now…"* She kindly requested to work in the field and also asked for her working hours to be extended. I guess you are getting the idea now. This is amazing, Ruth was truly dedicated to her job, and she knew that hard work pays in the end.

When true daughters and sons are working not resting at all times God rewards them. God sees and He is the Rewarder of them that *diligently* seek Him, (*Hebrews 11:6*). This means that as you work for the Lord, He simply blesses you because He can see your heart. *Galatians 6: 9*, *"And let us not be weary in well doing for in due season we shall reap, if we faint not."*

Remember she was just working in the field with the rest of Boaz's servants. I want to highlight something here so that you can understand. Boaz had his own appointed servants who were already working in his field. Bear in mind that Ruth wasn't part of his appointed servants who have been working since the harvest started. Notice that Ruth was humble enough to become a servant to Boaz. To be a true daughter or son it takes your submission as we said earlier. In other words, Ruth didn't have to wait for opportunity but she had to search for it. I can assume that Naomi could have planned a way for Ruth to get to know Boaz first so that she could glean in his fields. Notice that Ruth was well matured she knew the world of work. She knew the principles of getting into employment. Instead of the employer saying, "We are kindly recruiting workers; please call this number or contact so and so." Ruth just grabbed the opportunity. I believe Ruth just said to herself, "I know mum has done so much for me, so I don't want her to plan out how she can get me a job from Boaz." Grown up and matured daughters and sons simply reject the idea of being spoon fed. They learn to grow from circumstances they encounter in life.

She was now in the land, now it was her time to grow through serving. Servant stated here in case you might have a question. It means to become submissive to those above you, not thinking more highly of yourself than you ought but willing to serve as you grow from one level to another. Those who are willing to serve will excel, *John 13*. Watch the results of her humble character as we proceed with the story. *Servant*, this doesn't mean that you are now in bondage or oppressed by those above you. But you are embracing that moment as your time of exploration, a time of discovery and growing as you reach your goals spiritually. It can be a good practice, helping you to become humble and tender hearted to others around.

Galatians 5:13, "For, brethren, ye have been called unto liberty; only use not liberty for an occasion to the flesh, but by love serve one another."

You can create a good character of yourself, simply because it breaks pride and all behaviour that is associated with it. *Servant-hood/ sonship* is good for your growth if you want to develop or improve your standards in life.

Moreover, according to the book of Luke 15:11-32 we hear of the parable of the prodigal son. However, in this parable illustrates God's mercy on us as His children. In regards to the sonship, we realise that the young man after he had wasted all the resources he had, he remembered that going back to his father's house was the solution.

Luke 15: 17-18-19, *"And when he came to himself, he said, How many hired servants of my father's have bread enough and to spare, and I perish with hunger! (18) I will arise and go to my father, and will say unto him, Father, I have sinned against heaven, and before thee, (19) And am no more worthy to be called thy son: <u>make me as one of thy hired servants</u>."*

The scripture notifies us that this young man *remembered* that he needed to go back to his father and become a servant. In addition, becoming a servant in his father's house was a step forward of gaining humility and the willingness of becoming submissive to the instructions that he was going to receive. As we said earlier on that, servant-hood is a good solution of breaking pride and any character associated with it. *Philippians 2: 3, "Let nothing be done through strife or vainglory; but in lowliness of mind let each esteem other better than themselves."*

However the scripture also goes on to say,

Luke 15: 20-23, "And he arose, and came to his father. But when he was yet a great way off, his father saw him, and had compassion, and ran, and fell on his neck, and kissed him. (21) And the son said unto his Father, I have sinned against heaven, and in thy sight, and am no more worthy to be called thy son. (22) But the father said to his servants, Bring forth the best robe, and put it on him; and put a ring on his hand, and shoes on his feet: (23) And bring hither the fatted calf, and kill it; and let us eat and be merry:"

When this young man got rid of pride and any self-seeking character he was ready to fully walk in his sonship call. Sonship call is when one receives his or her spiritual parent who is there to guide and counsel an individual. This call can be fulfilled by breaking self-seeking behaviors that contradict humility or lowliness of the mind. Moreover, an individual can walk in his or her sonship call when he or she is willing to *step out* of disobedience. As we read the scripture above, we realise that this young man first walked out of shame, disobedience and he was willing to humble himself to the extent of becoming a servant. However, this suggests that servant-hood prepares an individual to fully walk in his or her sonship call in order to fulfill what God has ordained. By so doing it will lead to a brighter future. *Galatians 6:9, "And let us not be weary in well doing for in due season we shall reap, if we faint not."*

Chapter 7

Finds Favour...

Ruth 2: 8, "Then said Boaz unto Ruth, Hearest thou not, my daughter? Go not to glean in another field, neither go from hence, but abide here by my maidens: (9) Let thine eyes be on the field that they do reap, and go thou after them: have I not charged the young men that they shall not touch thee: and when thou art athirst, go unto the vessels, and drink of that which the young men have drawn. (10) Then she fell on her face, and bowed herself to the ground, and said unto him, Why have I found grace in thine eyes, that thou shouldest take knowledge of me, seeing I am a stranger? (11) And Boaz answered and said unto her, it hath fully been shewed me, all that thou hast done unto thy mother in law since the death of thine husband: and how thou hast left thy father and thy mother, and the land of thy nativity, and art come unto a people which thou knowest not heretofore."

Ruth finds favour in the sight of Boaz. As Ruth was dedicated to her work, doing all she can in the field, Boaz saw something unique in her. He saw true sonship character in her. Remember Ruth was just a foreigner though she told Naomi that her people were going to be her people, but still the rest of the city regarded her as a foreigner. Ruth joined the rest of the servants in the field, but Boaz noticed that there was something about her that he needed to know. He had to ask one of his servants, because Ruth was working hard.

Ruth found grace in his sight. Boaz could have lost his temper and kicked Ruth out of the fields saying, "Ah! Hey! Lady how come you are in my field, how can you employ yourself as if you own the field itself?" He could have cursed Ruth. See the favour of God upon Ruth's life. Ruth was courageous; she could have run away in fear when Boaz arrived in the field. Ruth stayed, she remained and she continued with her work as everyone else. She might have pretended as if she wasn't doing anything. Ruth knew that hard work pays in the end.

As we read the scripture, we hear that Boaz was talking to Ruth in a kind way. He was even treating her like his own daughter, with so much love and respect welcoming her into the new land.

Remember that Ruth was new in the land; she had no friends to talk to as everyone else. Begin to see the rewards of being a worker as you serve the Lord. Boaz told Ruth to abide or to stay with his maidens. Friends were added to her as she was busy working. *The benefits of becoming a servant of good tidings.* Not only Ruth received new friends, but Boaz had to command the young men not to touch her, but to respect and value her. Ruth was a woman of a noble character. She was fearfully and wonderfully made.

When the blessings are now pouring abundantly you end up getting confused whether you deserve them or not. You forget that previously you have been crying out that you may find favour. You begin to look at yourself thinking ah! Is what is happening here true or am I dreaming? You might even try to reverse the blessing saying, "May be someone else does deserve the blessing (removing yourself from it)." The scripture tells us that earlier on before Ruth went to the field, she said to Naomi, "Let me now go to the field, and glean ears of corn after him in whose sight I shall find grace."

Now, time came when Boaz had blessed Ruth with all his kind words of welcome, *Ruth fell on her face, and bowed herself to the ground, and said unto to him, Why have I found grace in thine eyes, that thou shouldest take knowledge of me, seeing I am a stranger?* After all that she said to Naomi earlier on, she is now appearing to be confused before Boaz of such favour she had received from him. You see, when a true daughter or son experiences triple or double portions of blessings they get confused. In other words, the blessings are too much to contain, to the extent that there will be no room enough to receive them. Ruth was simply touched by the way her simple prayer was answered. Remember she was now in the land of Judah.

Ruth 2: 12, "The Lord recompense thy work, and a full reward be given thee of the Lord God of Israel, under whose wings thou art come to trust."

Oh! What a blessing did Ruth receive; she found grace in his sight indeed. She therefore went on to say that, "She was comforted by his friendly words unto her." When you are a true son or daughter, the blessings will come your way unexpectedly. You just receive them and it's your right as a child of God to walk in favour.

You can go on and read the rest of the chapter. Read carefully and see the full reward she received.

Chapter 8

Act of Obedience...

Ruth 3:1, "Then Naomi her mother in law said unto her, My daughter, shall I not seek rest for thee, that it may be well with thee? (2) And now is not Boaz of our kindred, with whose maidens thou wast? Behold, he winnowed barley to night in the threshing-floor. (3) Wash thyself therefore, and anoint thee, and put thy raiment upon thee, and get thee down to the floor: but make not thyself known unto the man, until he shall have done eating and drinking. (4) And it shall be, when he lieth down, that thou shalt mark the place where he shall lie, and thou shalt go in, and uncover his feet, and lay thee down; and he will tell thee what thou shalt do. (5) And she said unto her, All that thou sayest unto me I will do

As we read the scripture above, it states that Naomi was instructing Ruth to go on the threshing-floor so that she could meet Boaz. Bear in mind that Naomi was her spiritual mother so, Ruth had to take the instruction and do in accordance to what she was told. This is a beautiful part of the story; remember Naomi has been with Ruth through thick and thin, even from Moab the country they left. Naomi has been watching Ruth. She saw her faithfulness to the vow she made; she saw how compassionate Ruth was to her and the sonship call that was within her. Listen to this, Ruth was willing to leave everything else for her spiritual mother, in addition all was well with her as long as Naomi was well secured. Ruth wasn't even thinking of leaving her spiritual mother for her benefit. She was a woman of a noble character and loyal.

I think you can now understand that Naomi's desire was for Ruth to flourish and bear good fruits. She didn't want her daughter to remain on the same level; she wanted Ruth to reach her destiny. I believe this is the heart of a spiritual parent. He or she wants to see their son or daughter progressing. Naomi wanted Ruth to stay where she was well looked after. She wanted Ruth to be treated as a lady because she knew that her daughter deserved better than where she was. I believe that Naomi just said to herself, "I have fought a good fight, I have been with my daughter and I have watched her grow as a virtuous woman and now, it is her time to start her new family *(new life)*." Moreover, Naomi knew that it was time for Ruth to reposition herself. That is what happens when true sons and daughters are moving from glory to glory. It is a joy for their spiritual parents to bless them. They will do everything they can to make sure that the daughter or son receives their portion.

Back to the story. In the scripture above Ruth was instructed to wash and perfume herself and put on the best clothes in preparation to receive her blessing. Note that when true sons and daughters are about to receive their portion, they don't just go and plan their route on their own. Their spiritual parents are there to assist and to make sure that the son or daughter is in the right position to take that which is theirs. I can imagine, Naomi running about buying all expensive designer clothing and perfume for her daughter. Maybe Ruth was just saying to herself, "Oh! How come Naomi today is joyous and saying all these unusual words to me. Maybe she forgot that I said I will be with her, and how come she now wants me to leave her and go to a home where I'm well provided for when I'm happy here where I am." I think all these thoughts were just running through her mind.

After Naomi instructed Ruth concerning everything that she needed to do, a polite and decent answer came out from Ruth's mouth. She said, *"All that thou sayest unto me I will do."* We can pause here. Was Ruth ready to do what she was told, though she answered to her spiritual mother that she was going to do *everything*?

Ruth could have questioned her mother in law and said all words of disobedience. Remember Naomi had the vision, she knew what she was talking about and she knew the outcome already *if she was going to obey*.

Was she willing to pass the test? This is what happens in most cases when spiritual parents instruct us to do something and we go in circles doing our own thing. Basically this means fulfilling our own desires that will make us fail to receive that which is ahead of us. Naomi saw the *bigger picture* ahead, she saw Ruth succeeding in the end. She saw Ruth in a bigger house with all that she required to sustain her. Naomi saw Ruth as a lender not a borrower; she saw her accomplishing big businesses and operating on top in the royal family. So, in most cases we tend to stick to our own preferences forgetting that God blessed us with spiritual parents so that they can help us fulfill our call. They are there to guide us and to shape us. Can you expect God to come down here on earth in person *(personally)* and start shaping you and making sure you get that which is ahead? Obviously the answer is "No!" God uses our spiritual parents to direct us. He speaks to them and they receive all instructions from Him.

As we all know Ruth was a wise woman. Though she was wise she needed instruction from her spiritual mother. This is what happens; when the sons and daughters get anointed they might think they can now operate in their own way. Meaning that they reject correction or instruction because of the anointing they have received through their spiritual parents. My point is no matter how strong and how anointed a son or daughter can be; they still need instruction from their spiritual parents. Remember as we said earlier on, that you have received an *impartation*, not the *whole of* it, but *a part of* the anointing. Ruth received instruction from her spiritual mother. I believe she could have said, "You are too old to give me an instruction, see things have changed now. We are no longer in the 80s, now the world has changed I can do my own thing mum." Ruth listened; she paid attention to the voice of her spiritual mother. She embraced her instruction. Let us see what happened next.

Ruth 3:6, "And she went down unto the floor, and did according to all that her mother in law bade her."

When Ruth had received the instruction from Naomi, the scripture states that, "she went down onto the floor, and *did according to all that her mother in law told her.*" Hallelujah! Ruth followed what she was told. True obedience should be seen in true sons and daughters. They do what they have been taught by their spiritual parents. They stick to that which they have received for the glory of God.

Now, that we have discussed the act *of obedience*, you can continue reading the story carefully. Let us find out what happens next when a true son or daughter is walking in obedience in the *next chapter.*

Chapter 9

Fruits of Obedience...

Ruth 4: 9, "And Boaz said unto the elders, and unto all the people, Ye are witnesses this day, that I have bought all that was Elimelech's and all that was Chilion's and Mahlon's of the hand of Naomi. (10) Moreover Ruth the Mobitess the wife of Mahlon, have I purchased to be my wife, to raise up the name of the dead upon his inheritance, that the name of the dead be not cut off from among his brethren, and from the gate of his place: ye are witnesses this day. (11) And all the people that were in the gate, and the elders, said, We are witnesses. The Lord make the woman that is come into thine house like Rachel and like Leah, which two did build the house of Israel: and do thou worthily in Ephratah, and be famous in Bethlehem: (12) And let thy house be like the house of Pharez, whom Tamar bare unto Judah, of the seed which the Lord shall give thee of this young woman."

The moment you *obey* everything flows. I believe Ruth didn't know what was going to happen in the end. She just followed the instructions like her spiritual mother had told her. Remember she didn't question her when she was being instructed. Ruth took a step of obedience.

When you finally take that step of obedience, in most cases you don't know what is ahead but you just decide to listen anyway. Just like Ruth, she didn't know that her obedience was leading her to her destiny. Maybe Ruth was curious of what was going to happen in the end. As we all know that when you have been instructed to do something you become curious to the extent that you want to know the outcome of it there and then (without delay). Well! Ruth kept calm and just

Obedience to Sonship Call

accomplished the assignment without worrying about the outcome. Ruth could have changed the plan and did it the other way round and satisfied her desires. But the good thing is that, Ruth remained persistent, she followed the instructions. Naomi knew that Ruth was going to finish the task very well, she knew her daughter.

Naomi could have followed Ruth to make sure she did the right thing, but she waited at home in faith that Ruth was going to complete the task well. You see now, as a daughter or son of your spiritual parents there is a time when they will leave you to go and accomplish a task, in other words they may send you to collect that which belongs to you instead of them doing it for you. It will be a time for you to *prove* how *mature* you are and *faithful* you are to remain *obedient* to that which you have been instructed. This doesn't mean that your spiritual parent is not with you at that time. In most cases I believe that, they will be praying on your behalf so that you may do the right thing. I can imagine, Naomi praying to God for protection and guidance upon Ruth in her closet. You see! *That is the heart of a spiritual parent.* They pray for you on your behalf, so that you may receive your spiritual inheritance. Now, the question is how faithful and how obedient are you to follow instructions you are given? In other words, when your spiritual father or mother says go right, are you willing to do that and not go to your left?

Back to our story. We hear that Ruth did *exactly* what she was told and she came back home and gave detail of everything that took place to her spiritual mother. She could have hidden some of the information but Ruth told her *every detail.* Hallelujah!

As we read the scripture, note that when you are walking in obedience to the Word of God things just flow. Furthermore, blessings run to you automatically and you don't need to negotiate. Not only will those who are close to you witness your success but people around (the ones you don't even know) will also celebrate your success. They will come together and witness the goodness of the Lord in your life. Indeed our God will even reward His people openly. Let us read again this scripture on Ruth 4:11-12...

(11) And all the people that were in the gate, and the elders, said, We are witnesses. The Lord make the woman that is come into thine house like Rachel and like Leah, which two did build the house of Israel: and do thou worthily in Ephratah, and be famous in Bethlehem: (12) And let thy house be like the house of Pharez, whom Tamar bare unto Judah, of the seed which the Lord shall give thee of this young woman."

Some people, who didn't even know Ruth personally, just came to witness. They also spoke blessings upon her life, welcoming her into the land. I just felt that this time, it was now her *official welcome*, not just an ordinary welcome into the land but also in the spiritual realm. She was now officially received by the people of the foreign land, the people of Judah who lived in that country. I believe her contract with Naomi was being fulfilled, remember Ruth made a *vow*. Everyone was there to receive her. She completed her mission successfully. Ruth and Naomi fought a good fight; it was the fight of faith. They maintained their relationship till the end. Bear in mind that, *without Naomi, there is no success in Ruth's life.*

Ruth's obedience to Naomi and unto God, made her excel. She received the sonship call through obedience. She followed the instructions and she obeyed. Ruth obeyed the voice of the Lord through her spiritual mother. The blessing was also for the next generations to come. Boaz married Ruth and she gave birth to a son called Obed.

The Holy Spirit just touched my heart as I'm writing, let us pause here. Obed, I would like to believe that the name Obed comes from or has been taken from the word "Obedience"_ Obed-ience, Obedience. It takes obedience for you to receive your portion in the Lord. I would like to believe that God caused them to give their child the name "Obed" because it was through Ruth's *obedience* to *sonship call* for her to conquer and became a victor. Just to highlight or add on something here, other studies or research also confirm that the name Obed means a *servant or workman*. Bear in mind as we said earlier on that, to achieve *obedience* and to effectively walk in your *sonship call* you have to be *willing* to become a *servant or a workman* and in due season you will reap if you faint not *(Galatians 6:9)*. The name Obed is not an ordinary name, I now get the picture. *(Everything just flows, there is a connection)*. Her son Obed can also represent *an award* that Ruth received in the end of the *test* of Obedience *to Sonship Call,* Ruth had to get her reward. She had to receive Obed in order for her to *remember* that it was through *obedience* that made her *excel.*

Remember, Ruth was a worker *(workman),* therefore since it was in her system; she had to pass on the seed of hard work, a seed of obedience *(Obed). From generation to generation.* You can even read on and on if you want to get the results or the full package of what and who came after her. Well! Let it be an encouragement to me and you to pass a good seed, a seed of excellence to the next generation. God is so good! She received a *son;* moreover to me it is confirmation of the message, *Sonship call.* Child of God, *Obedience to Sonship Call, Obedience to Sonship Call,* receive the call in your spirit, there are greater things ahead. Keep pressing on.

Philippians 3:13-14, "(13)Brethren, I count not myself to have apprehended: <u>but this one thing I do, forgetting those things which are behind, and reaching forth unto those things which are before, (14)I press toward the mark for the prize of the high calling of God in Christ Jesus.</u>"

Overflowing blessings indeed. Obed became the father of Jesse. Jesse became also the father of David, Ah! You see where the story is going now. This is amazing, it goes on and on. Ruth became the great grandmother of Jesus Christ. Oh! Just give God all the praise! Indeed it is a lovely story, fully packed with a powerful revelation. *The fruits of Obedience.*

Chapter 10

Conclusion

I believe that you have been blessed with this message of *Obedience to Sonship Call*. It is a call that is fulfilled or will fully be active in you the moment you become obedient to the one who is above you *(spiritual parent)* and unto God. I understand that since we have gone through the book of Ruth we find in the Bible, you now know what it means when someone is *above* you. In other words, you have an idea of what it means when you obey and become submissive to the instructions you receive from the one who is there to stir your calling in the Lord.

The story of Ruth clearly demonstrates *the power of obedience* and its impact upon our lives in shaping the inner man. If the inner man is truly submissive to the call of the Lord through our spiritual parents, we can reach our spiritual destiny. We can get where God expects us to be.

Sonship call prepares our hearts to desire that which God has set for our lives. Through listening and paying attention to the words of wisdom given by our spiritual parents *in the Lord*, we can gain access to our destiny. Sonship call helps us to stay connected to our spiritual parents so that we can receive our blessings from the Lord. Remember as we have discussed in the chapters, that without Naomi there is no progress in Ruth's life. In other words, for Ruth to excel Naomi should be there to direct her paths leading to a successful life. I understand that Ruth on her own could not gain all that she required, so she needed Naomi to direct her paths. Naomi had a bigger picture, she saw the picture ahead. Oh! This is an interesting story. It is the story of *Obedience to Sonship Call*.

Oh! I believe that you are getting the picture. When God places that sonship call in your spirit, will you be able to remain obedient to the call? Obedience can only be fulfilled when you accept the call you have received, by humbling yourself to become a servant/a workman who is willing to serve in the ministry.

I believe most of us do go to Church, I mean going to our local places of worship where we meet up as a group in agreement to worship and praise God. Well! The point is, whilst you are in that Church or Assembly, are you willing to serve? Not just enjoying and warming the chairs or benches and going back home saying, I have been blessed. In other words, are you willing to work in the house of the Lord and support the ministry or the vision that your spiritual parent has received for your benefit. Perhaps you expect the chairs to be arranged for you, and all instruments to be set so that you can just come and raise your hands in worship and praise. Well! Allow me to explain to you, that as we come to the Lord in respective places of worship, God expects us to be the workers. He expects us to work effectively and support His vision He has given our spiritual parents to lead. I know now you might be wondering, "But we only go to church to get blessed." Well! There is nothing wrong with that, it's true, we go to church to get blessed. But, true sons and daughters look for opportunities, sitting down and folding arms and waiting to be blessed is not their portion. They are willing to serve as they receive their blessing. In addition, this is the sonship call active in their inner man.

I believe that as you were reading this book, you have been transformed inside out. It is your season child of God! Receive your blessing as you make that sonship call you have received deep within *active*, and as you *obey* your spiritual parents. Take each instruction and your life will never be the same again. Be the true son or daughter. Be willing to *serve*; don't expect blessings to just come on your way when you are not willing to work as you support the work of God. Furthermore, be a blessing and be the partaker of good things. You can now go an extra mile serving the Lord with all your heart, mind and soul, Hallelujah!

To God be the Glory. Thank you for taking this opportunity to read this book. I believe that you have been inspired to walk in *obedience*. It doesn't matter how long it will take for you to reach your destiny but, keep on serving and keep on obeying. God will reward you in due season. May the Lord Almighty, The One who is Worthy of all the praise and worship bless you more! Hallelujah!

Image by: Kundai Valentine Murefu

Lightning Source UK Ltd.
Milton Keynes UK
UKOW04f2300310315

248891UK00002B/98/P